**Featuring the contributions of:**

*MARGARET BRUNER*
*GEOFFREY CHAUCER*
*EMILY DICKINSON*
*BENJAMIN FRANKLIN*
*SIR ALEXANDER GRAY*
*EDWARD LEAR    ALEXANDER POPE*
*CARL SANDBURG*
*SIR WALTER SCOTT*
*JONATHAN SWIFT*
*ADLAI STEVENSON*
*MARK TWAIN*

*and* **oodles** *and* **oodles of others**

Library of Congress Catalog Card
# 94-75719

ISBN 0-9622873-1-8

Printed in USA by Griffin Printing
Sacramento, California

Gordon Publishing
91 Jane Ann Way
Campbell CA 95008-2712

**Other books:**

**Guide to Mexico's Copper Canyon**

ISBN 0-9622873-0-X

Hugger's favorite

# CATQUOTES and *ANECDOTES*, *ETC.*, *Etc.*, *etc.*

## Proverbs, poems, limericks, rhymes, quotes, and anecdotes about cats

*compiled and photographed by Richard Gordon*

## GORDON PUBLISHING
## 91 JANE ANN WAY, CAMPBELL CA 95008-2712

# CONTENTS

Poems:

I'm six weeks old, orphaned, nameless, and cooped up in a cage at the  animal shelter.  A guy walks by.  I stick out my paw and snag his sweater.  He reads the sign tacked to the front of my cage.

"This sign says, 'Hugs and Kisses,'" he says  to the attendant. "What's that all about?"

"I'll show you," she says.  She takes me out of the cage and puts me on her chest.  I'm hungry for food and warmth so I reach out my paws toward her shoulders and start to nibble her chin.

"I'll take it," says the guy.

"It ain't an it," says the girl.  "It's a boy."

He takes me home and names me Hugger.

Now I live in a house instead of a cage.  I sleep days, ram around nights, and eat incessantly.  I knock pencils, pens, erasers and paper clips off from tables on to the floor.

My look-alike ancestors (well, almost look-alike--my

tail isn't normal--it curls along one side) appeared about ten million years ago and continue almost unchanged in the modern world.

Ancient Egyptians considered us sacred. Anyone who killed a cat, even accidentally, was put to death.

The Romans considered us a symbol of freedom and a cat stood at the feet of the Goddess of Liberty.

Superstitious people in Medieval times thought my black cousins were demons in disguise and witches' companions.

But--today, dogs take second place; cats are the favorite household pet.

Here are my favorite catquotes, anecdotes, proverbs, poetry, limericks, and nursery rhymes. I hope you enjoy them.

(Hugger)

2

**CAT:** A miniature tiger kept in a home to remind children to wash their faces.

*Anonymous*

God created the cat that man might have the pleasure of caressing a tiger.

*Korea (artist unknown)*

*Ferdinand Mery (1897-1964)*

3

*When I play with my cat, who knows if I am not a pastime to her more than she is to me.*

Michel Eyquem de Montaigne (1533-1592)

*One of the most striking differences between a cat and a lie is that the cat has only nine lives.*

Mark Twain (1835-1910)

Ah! Cats are a mysterious kind of folk. There is more passing in their minds than we are aware of. It comes no doubt from their being so familiar with warlocks and witches.

Sir Walter Scott (1771-1832)

Dogs come when they're called; cats take a message and get back to you.

Mary Bly

8

*A kitten is so flexible that she is almost double; the hind parts are equivalent to another kitten with which the forepart plays. She does not discover that her tail belongs to her until you tread upon it.*

*Henry David Thoreau (1817-62)*

9

We should be careful to get out of an experience only the wisdom that is in it-- and stop there: lest like the cat that sits down on a hot stove lid.  She will never sit down on a hot stove lid again--and that is well, but also she will never sit down on a cold one anymore.

Mark Twain (1835-1910)

*Of all of God's creatures there is only one that cannot be made the slave of the lash. That one is the cat. If man could be crossed with a cat it would improve man, but it would deteriorate the cat.*

*Mark Twain. (1835-1910)*
*(Sketch Seattle Post-Intelligencer 14 Sept. 1895)*

*The cat in gloves catches no mice.*

Benjamin Franklin's <u>Poor Richard's Almanac</u>

*Ignorant people think it's the noise which fighting cats make that is so aggravating, but it ain't so; it's the grammar they use.*

Mark Twain (1835-1910)

12

Cats are smarter than dogs.  You can't get eight cats to pull a sled through snow.

Jeff Valdez

Cat:  A quadruped, the legs, as usual, being at the four corners.

Anonymous

*But thousands die of this or that;*
*Die, and endow a college or a cat.*

Alexander Pope (1688-1744)

(More than 200 years later, cats are still being endowed. In May of 1993, Ann Morgan of Seattle, Washington passed away. Her will leaves $500,000 to Tinker, her white Turkish Angora-type cat. She describes Tinker as being her best friend and companion and mandates that her apartment be maintained and a caretaker be hired to provide for him in her absence. The balance of her estate goes to charity.)

*All dogs look up to you.*
*All cats look down on you.*
*Only a pig looks at you as an*
*equal.*

(attrib.) Winston Churchill (1874-1965)

*Cats are like Baptists. They raise*
*hell but you can't catch them at it.*

Anonymous

*Cats like men are flatterers.*

*Walter Savage Landor (1824-53)*

*An example of sophistication minus civilization.*

*Anonymous*

*To err is human.  To purr is feline.*

*Robert Byrne*

And he (a cat) is a full lecherouse beast in youthe: swyfte, plyaunt and mery, and lepyth and restyth on all thynge that is tofore him. And is led by a straw and playeth therwyth.

The Tale of Beryn c 1400

"I have just been given a very engaging Persian Kitten ... and his opinion is that I should have been given to him."

Letters Evelyn Underhill (1875-1941)

18

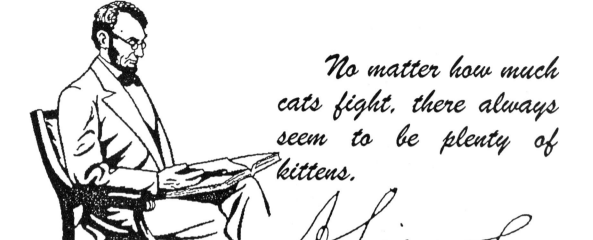

*No matter how much cats fight, there always seem to be plenty of kittens.*

*A Lincoln*

*1809-1865*

*It's better to be a mouse in a cat's mouth than a man in a lawyer's hands.*

*Spanish proverb*

19

*Nothing is more playful than a young cat, nor more grave than an old one.*

Thomas Fuller (1654-1734)

*Thou art the Great Cat, the avenger of the Gods, and the judge of words, and the president of the sovereign chiefs, and the governor of the holy Circle; thou art indeed...the Great Cat.*

*Inscription on the royal tombs at Thebes*

*One cat just leads to another.*

Ernest Hemingway (1898-1967)

*A man has to work so hard so that something of his personality stays alive. A tomcat has it easy, he has only to spray and his presence is there for years on rainy days.*

Albert Einstein (1879-1955)

*I've met with thinkers and many cats, but the wisdom of cats is infinitely superior.*

Hippolyte Taine (1828-1893)

*A young cat or kitten is graceful; her chief occupation is chasing her tail, but her tail will not stay chased.*

Edgar Allen Poe (1809-1849)

*I had rather be a kitten and cry mew...*

William Shakespeare (1564-1616)

Henry IV, Part One

The Mouse should stand in Feare.
So should the squeaking Rat;
All this would I doe if I were
Converted to a Cat.

Geroge Turberville (ca 1540-1610)

A home without a cat--a well-fed,
well-petted, and properly-revered cat--
may be a perfect home, perhaps, but how
can it prove its title?

Mark Twain (1835-1910)

Cat mighty dignified till de dog come by.

American Negro proverb

Cats, flies, and women are ever at their toilets.

French proverb

The three merriest things in the world are a cat's kitten, a goat's kid, and a young widow.

Irish proverb

24

A lame cat is better than a swift horse when rats infest the palace.

Chinese proverb

To live long; eat like a cat, drink like a dog.

German proverb

Never try to catch a black cat at night.

Liberian proberb

You've read my
favorite quotes.
Here are my favorite

*Anecdotes:*

Sir Isaac Newton cut a hole in the bottom of an outside door so that he wouldn't be bothered when his cat wanted in or out.

The cat had kittens whereupon Newton (it is reported) cut a small hole next to the original one.

A friend was very upset at having to get rid of his cat. "Have you tried curiosity?" asked writer/critic Dorothy Parker.

Dorothy Parker (1893-1967)

"If cats were born in an oven, wud they be biscuits?" argued Finley Peter Dunne. Nevertheless the Supreme court held (in United States v Wong Kim Ark 1898) that all Chinese who were born in the United States were citizens.

Once upon a time, a monkey who wanted to get some roasting chestnuts from the fire used the paw of his friend, the cat.

(Today, a person employed to perform a difficult or dangerous job is called a "cat's paw" and the service is referred to as "pulling chestnuts out of the fire.")

President Coolidge invited friends from Vermont to dine at the White House. Worried lest they make a mistake in table manners, they decided to watch Cal and do as he did. When Cal poured his coffee into his saucer, they did the same; when he added sugar and cream to the coffee in the saucer, they did the same. The president then placed the saucer of coffee on the floor for the cat.

*Anonymous*

32

Anxious about Kali's cross-country flight to the home of our daughter, I called the airlines.

"Don't worry," the witty baggage clerk reassured me, "Kali will be eating gourmet salmon and watching Garfield movies all the way from San Francisco to Boston."

Ethel Kessler (1921-)

## Kevin Barry (1902-1920)

Among the many crimes put down to this dangerous man is that he did put pepper in the cat's milk and steal a penny from a blind man; besides, he wilfully, feloniously and of malice aforethought did smile derisively at a policeman.

Written on the eve of his execution, 31 October 1920

Cats and people are funny animals. Cats have four paws and only one maw. People have forefathers and only one mother.

When a cat smells a rat, he gets excited--so do people. Cats carry tails, and lots of people carry tales too. All cats have fur coats.

Some people who don't have fur coats say catty things about the ones that have them.

*Essay by an unknown, precocious grade school student*

"What's your kitty's name?" asked the woman.

"Ben Hur," answered Jimmy.

"That's a funny name for a cat. Why did you name it that?"

"Well, we just called him Ben until he had kittens."

Anonymous

"I've just run over your cat. I'm sorry. I want to replace him," said the concientious motorist to the lady at the farmhouse door.

"Good," replied the farmer's wife. "Get busy. There's a mouse in the pantry right now."

Anonymous

A mouse took a few licks of some whiskey the farmer spilled on the barn floor. The mouse liked the taste. He took a few more licks, and then even some more. When the liquor began to take effect, he puffed out his chest, got up on his hind legs, and hollered, "Now bring on that damned cat!"

Anonymous

"*I cannot agree that it should be the declared public policy of Illinois that a cat visiting a neighbor's yard or crossing the highway is a public nuisance. It is in the nature of cats to do a certain amount of unescorted roaming ... to escort a cat abroad on a leash is against the nature of the owner. Moreover, cats perform useful service, particularly in the rural areas.*

The problem of the cat vs. the bird is as old as time.  If we attempt to resolve it by legislation, ... we may be called up to take sides as well in the age-old problems of dog vs. cat, bird vs. bird, or even bird vs. worm. In my   opinion the State of Illinois and its local governing bodies already have enough to do without trying to control feline delinquency.

In message to Illinois Senate, Adlai Stevenson (1835-1914)

Once upon a time, mother mouse and baby mouse were being chased by the family cat. Suddenly mother turned and barked out in her loudest voice, "Bow-wow!"

The frightened cat ran away. Turning to her baby, mother mouse said, "Now you see the advantage of a second language."

Anonymous

41

*Poems:*

# Cat

A pet who sleeps away
A goodly portion of the day
So he can prowl around and fight
When we would like to sleep at night.

Richard Wheeler (1922--)

When tea is brought at five o'clock
And all the curtains drawn with care,
The little black cat with bright green eyes
Is suddenly purring there.

Harold Munro (1879-1932)

## Muse versus Mews

Sometimes when I have racked my brain
In writing sonnet or quatrain,
My cat lies curled up like a ball,
Asleep, oblivious to it all.
And then perhaps at last when I
Achieve my aim and breathe a sigh
Of gratitude, she wakes and views
Me wonderingly, as if the muse
Were something she would hardly deem
As worth while, say--as meat or cream,
And languidly she eyes my sonnet
Then stretches and sits down upon it.

Margaret E. Bruner (1866-1971)

# Fog

The fog comes
on little cat feet.
It sits looking
over the harbor and city
on silent haunches
and then moves on.

Carl Sandburg (1878-1967)

# Tiberius

Cruel, but composed and bland,
Dumb, inscrutable and grand,
So Tiberius might have sat,
Had Tiberius been a cat.

Mathew Arnold (1822-88)


# Cruel Clever Sally

Sally, having swallowed cheese,
Directs down holes the scented breeze
Enticing thus with baited breath
Nice mice to an untimely death.

Geoffrey Taylor

Said the cat, and he was Manx,
   "Oh, Captain Noah, wait!
I'll catch the mice to give you thanks,
   And pay for being late."
So the cat got in, but oh,
His tail was a bit too slow.

Old English

I don't care much for the people
Who are living with me in this house,
But I own that I love a good fire
And an occasional herring and mouse.

C. B. Cranch (1813-1892)

### Under the Table Manners

It's hard to be polite
    If you're a cat.
When other folk are up at the table
Eating all that they are able
    You are down on the mat
    If you're a cat.

You're expected just to sit
    If you're a cat,
Not to let them know you're there

By scratching at the chair
    Or with light respectful pat
    If you're a cat.

You are not to make a fuss
    If you're a cat
Tho' there's fish upon the plate
You're expected just to wait.
    Wait prettily on the mat
    If you're a cat.

*Anonymous*

# The Duel

The gingham dog and the
    calico cat
Side by side on the table sat;
'Twas half-past twelve,
    and (what do you think!)
Nor one nor t'other
    had slept a wink!

The Old Dutch clock
    and the Chinese plate
Appeared to know
    as sure as fate
There was going to be
    a terrible spat.
(I wasn't there, I simply state
What was told to me
    by the Chinese plate!)

Eugene Field (1850-1895)

# Montague Michael

Montague Michael
You're much too fat,
You wicked old, wily old,
Well-fed cat.

All night you sleep
On a cushion of silk,
And twice a day
I bring you milk.

53

### A Cat's Conscience

A dog will often steal a bone,
But conscience lets him not alone,
And by his tail his guilt is known.

But cats consider theft a game,
And, howsoever you may blame,
Refuse the slightest sign of shame.

*Anonymous*

And once in a while,
When you catch a mouse,
You're the proudest person
In all the house.

But spoilt as you are,
I tell you, Cat,
This chair is all mine
And you can't have that!

*Anonymous*

My kitty cat has nine lives.
Yes, nine long lives has she.
Three to spend in eating,
Three to spend in sleeping,
And three to spend up the Chestnut tree.

Anonymous

55

Diamond Cut Diamond

Two cats
One up a tree
One under a tree
The cat up a tree is a he
The cat under the tree is a she
The tree is witch elm, just incidentally.
He takes no notice of she, she take no notice of he.
He stares at the woolly clouds passing, she stares at the tree.
There's been a lot written about cats, by Old Possum, Yeats and Company
But not Alfred de Musset or Lord Tennyson or Poe or anybody
Write about one cat under, and one cat up, a tree.
God knows why this should be left for me
Except I like cats as cats be
Especially one cat up
And one cat under
A witch elm
Tree.

Ewart Milne (1903-87)

# Pangor Ban

I and Pangor Ban, my cat,
'Tis a like task we are at;
Hunting mice is his delight,
Hunting words I sit all night.

So in peace our tasks we ply,
Pangor Ban, my cat and I;
In our arts we find our bliss
I have mine and he has his.

Unknown Irish Monk (8th Century)

I like little Pussy, her coat is so warm,

And if I don't hurt her, she'll do me no harm.

So I'll not pull her tail, nor drive her away

But Pussy and I very gently will play.

Jane Taylor (1783-1824)

Two wymen in one howse;
Two cattes and one mowce;
Two dogges and one bone;
Maye never accorde in one.

Old English

To Banbury came I, Oh Profane-one,
Where I saw a Puritan-one
Hanging his cat on Monday
For killing a mouse on Sunday.

Richard Brathwaite (1588-1673)

# In Memorian Leo: A Yellow Cat

Whisper some kindly word, to bless
A wistful soul who understands
That life is but one long caress
Of gentle words and gentle hands.

*Margaret P. Sherwood (1864-1955)*

My mistress turned into a ghost,
I reign supreme and rule the roast;
Yet I cannot claim to be
Half so great a cat as she.

*Martin Armstrong (1882-1974)*

The Kitten, how she starts,
Crouches, stretches, paws, and darts!
Were her antics played in the eye
Of a thousand standers-by,
Clapping hands with shout and stare,
What would little Tabby care
For the plaudits of the crowd?
Over happy to be proud,
Over wealthy in the treasure
Of her own exceeding pleasure!

William Wordsworth (1770-1850)

# Tabatha Jane

I am a very old pussy,
    My name is Tabitha Jane;
I've had about fifty kittens,
    So I think I mustn't complain...
Now I think I have a right,
    being aged,
    To take an old tabby's repose;
To have a good breakfast
    and dinner,
    And to sit by the fire and doze.

Anonymous

# The Cat

Observe the Cat upon this page.
Philosophers in every age,
The very wisest of the wise
Have tried her mind to analyze
In vain, for nothing can they learn.
She baffles them at every turn
Like Mister Hamlet in the play.
She leads their reasoning astray;

She feigns an interest in string
Or yarn or any rolling thing.
Unlike the Dog, she does not care
With common Man her thoughts to
share.
She teaches us that in life's walk
'T is better to let others talk,
And listen while they say instead
The foolish things we might have said.

Oliver Herford (1863-1935)

## On a Cat, Ageing

He blinks upon the hearth-rug,
And yawns in deep content,
Accepting all the comforts
That Providence has sent.

Louder he purrs and louder,
In one glad hymn of praise
For all the night's adventures,
For quietful restful days.

Life will go on forever,
    With all that cat can wish;
Warmth and the glad procession
    Of fish and milk and fish.

Only--the thought disturbs him--
    He's noticed once or twice,
The times are somehow breeding
    A nimbler race of mice.

Sir Alexander Gray (1882-1968)

68

# Familiarity Dangerous

As in her ancient mistress' lap,
 The youthful tabby lay,
They gave each other many a tap,
 Alike dispos'd to play.

But strife ensues.  Puss waxes warm,
 And with protruded claws
Ploughs all the length of Lydia's arm,
 Mere wantonness the cause.

At once, resentful of the deed,
　　She shakes her to the ground
With many a threat, that she shall bleed
　　With still a deeper wound.

But, Lydia, bid thy fury rest!
　　It was a venial stroke;
For she, that will with kittens jest,
　　Should bear a kitten's joke.

William Cowper (1731-1800)

# That Cat

The cat that comes to my window sill
When the moon looks cold and the night is still--
He comes in a frenzied state alone
With a tail that stands like a pine tree cone,
And says, "I have finished my evening lark,
My whiskers are froze'nd and stuck to my chin.
I do wish you'd git up and let me in."
                    That cat gits in.

But if in the solitude of the night
He doesn't appear to be feeling right,
And rises and stretches and seeks the floor,
And some remote corner he would explore,
And doesn't feel satisfied just because
There's no good spot for to sharpen his claws,
And meows and canters uneasy about
Beyond the least shadow of any doubt
                    That cat gits out.

Ben King (1857-94)

72

When food mysteriously goes,
The chances are that Pussy knows
More than she leads you to suppose.

And hence there is no need for you,
If Puss declines a meal or two,
To feel her pulse and make ado.

                                    *Anonymous*

Oh cat of Churlish kind,
The fiend was in thy mind
When thou my bird entwined.

John Skelton (1460-1529)

Cats may have their goose
Cooked by tobacco juice.
Still why deny its use
Thoughtfully taken.

C. S. Calverley (1831-84)

## Cat's Taste

Our cat likes her menu rich
With carp, cod, lobster,
   crab and 'sich'
A bit of caviar to add
   to her fish --
Or any other tasty dish!

R. Day (1913-) and
S. Day (1925-)

# The Kitten At Play

See the kitten on the wall,
Sporting with the leaves that fall,
Withered leaves, one, two and three
Falling from the elder tree,
Through the calm and frosty air
Of the morning bright and fair.

See the kitten, how she starts,
Crouches, stretches, paws and darts;
With a tiger-leap half way

Now she meets her coming prey.
Lets it go as fast and then
Has it in her power again.

Now she works with three and four,
Like and Indian conjurer;
Quick as he in feats of art,
Gracefully she plays her part;
Yet were gazing thousands there;
What would little Tabby care?

William Wordsworth (1770-1850)

80

# She Sights a Bird

She sights a Bird--she chuckles--
She flattens--then she crawls--
She runs without the look of feet--
Her eyes increase to Balls--

Her Jaws stir--twitching--hungry--
Her Teeth can hardly stand--
She leaps, but Robin leaped the first--
Ah, Pussy, of the Sand,

The Hopes so juicy ripening--
You almost bathed your Tongue--
When Bliss disclosed a hundred Toes--
And fled with ever one--

Emily Dickinson (1830-86)


Careful observers may foretell the hour
(By sure prognostics) when to dread a show'r.
While rain depends, the pensive cat gives o'er
Her frolics and pursues her tail no more.

Jonathan Swift (1667-1745)

# To a Cat

Stately, kindly, lordly friend,
  Condescend
Here to sit by me, and turn
Glorious eyes that smile and burn,
Golden eyes, love's lustrous meed,
On the golden page I read.

All your wondrous wealth of hair,
  Dark and fair,
Silken-shaggy, soft and bright

As the clouds and beams of night,
Pays my reverent hand's caress
Back with friendlier gentleness.

Dogs may fawn on all and some
    As they come;
You, a friend of loftier mind,
Answer friends alone in kind.
Just your foot upon my hand
Softly bids it understand.

Algernon Charles Swinburne (1837-1909)

*Gather Kittens while you may,*
*Time brings only Sorrow;*
*And the Kittens of To-day*
*Will be Old Cats To-morrow.*

Oliver Herford (1863-1935)

*Starving Cat (Artist Unknown)*

# Bathsheba

Bathsheba! to whom none ever said scat—
No worthier cat
Ever sat on a mat,
Or caught a rat.
Requies---cat!

John Greenleaf Whittier (1807-92)

Let take a cat, and fostre him wel with milk
And tendre flesh, and make his couche of silk,
And lat him see a mouse go by the wal
Anon he weyveth milk, and flesh, and al
And every deyntee which is in that hous,
Swich appetyt hath he to ete a mous.

Manciple's Tale, Geoffrey Chaucer (1340?-1400)

## Stanley, The Aristocrat

Feathers
Of wren, about,
As regal, black feline
Licks lips, cleans fur, rejects cat food
Blackguard!

Eulah H. Blaine (1910-)

## Black Cat

Black cat, black cat--
when he cross yo' track.
No matter what you gwine.
To a dippin' or a dyin'
No matter whar you huryin'
You better turn back.

*Anonymous*

*Limericks:*

There wanst was two cats of Kilkenny.
And aich thought there was wan cat too
many;
        So they quarrelled and they bit,
        'Til barrin' their nails
        And the tips of their tail
Instead of two cats, there warn't any.

(The expression "to fight like two cats of Kilkenny" meaning "to fight until both sides are done in" is explained thus: During the Irish rebellion of 1798 a group of Hessian soldiers was garrisoned in Kilkenny. A Hessian tried to amuse himself by tying the tails of two cats together and throwing the cats over a clothesline to fight. When an officer approached, the Hessian cut the two tails with his sword and the cats bolted. Asked to explain the two bleeding tails, he explained to the officer that two cats had been fighting and had devoured all of each other except their bleeding tails.)

There was a bald man with a cat
That he wore around town as a hat
    Until one night, blind drunk
    He got hold of a skunk
And that was the end of all that.

Max Gordon (1946-)

There was a young man from the city
Who saw what he thought was a kitty.
To make sure of that
He gave it a pat.
They buried his clothes--what a pity!

Anonymous

Said a cat as he looked at the king,
"You're really an impossible thing.
You're suffering from hives,
While I'm living nine lives.
What a pity, you old Ding-a-ling!"

Richard Gordon (1917-)

(That "a cat has nine lives" probably derives from the cat's ability to land on four feet when dropped or tossed from a height that would mean death to any other animal.

The cat has a 13 to 17 year life span. Thus it is the longest-lived small domestic animal. Mixed-breed cats tend to outlive purebreds by three months to one year.)

Said a cat as he playfully threw
His wife down a well in Peru.
    "Relax, dearest Dora
    Please don't be angora
I only was artesian you"

Unknown

A cat in despondency sighed
And resolved to commit suicide
    She passed under the wheels
    Of eight automobiles
And under the ninth one she died.

Anonymous

There was a kind curate of Kew
Who kept a large cat in a pew.
    There he taught it each week
    A new letter of Greek,
But it never got further than <u>Mu</u>.

<u>Lots of Limericks</u>, Louis Untermeyer, ed.

As the fiddler sawed "Do, Re, Mi,"
A cat sharpened claws on his knee.
Said the man to the cat,
"Just once more like that,
I'll string you and tune you to G."

Richard Gordon (1917-)

(Just kidding--violin strings are made of catgut, but catgut has never been made from cats. Catgut is made from sheep intestine.)

Of a sudden the great prima donna
Cried, "Gawd, but my voice is a
goner!"
    But a cat in the wings
    Said, "I know how she sings,"
And finished the solo with honor.

Anonymous

There was an old spinster from Fife
Who had never been kissed in her life;
    Along came a cat
    And she said, "I'll kiss that!"
But the cat meowed, "Not on your
life!"

Anonymous

There was an Old Man on the Border
Who lived in the utmost disorder;
 He danced with the Cat
 And made tea in his Hat
Which vexed all the folks on the Border.

Edward Lear (1812-88)

*Tillie, my cat, loves to preen.*
*She struts around like a queen.*
*Sometimes she acts good,*
*Then not as she should.*
*Her true nature lies in between.*

*Seth Hudson (1976-)*

105

I once owned a cat name of Fred.
"My needs are quite simple," he said.
"A scratch on the head,
The prime spot in bed,
Remember your place; I'm purebred."

Richard Gordon (1917-)

Nursery Rhymes:

We are all in the dumps,
For diamonds are trumps;
The kittens are gone to St. Pauls,
The babies are bit,
The moon's in a fit
And the houses are built without walls.

Pussy cat, pussy cat, where have you been?
I've been to London to look at the queen.
Pussy cat, pussy cat, what did you there?
I frightened a little mouse under her chair.

## Oh, Lovely, Lovely, Lovely

The witch flew out on Halloween,
Her hair was blue, her nose was green,
Her teeth the longest ever seen,
Oh, she was lovely, lovely, lovely!

Her cat was black and fit and fat,
He lashed his tail and humped his back,

He scritched and scratched and hissed
    and spat.
Oh, he was lovely, lovely, lovely!

They rode a cleaner, not a broom.
"Go left!" screeched the Puss and spoke
    their doom.
She turned right--they hit the moon.
Oh, it was lovely, lovely, lovely

Three little kittens
They lost their mittens,
And they began to cry.
Oh mother dear,
We sadly fear
Our mittens we have lost.
What! lost your mittens
You naughty kittens!
Then you shall have no pie.

Attributed to Eliza Lee Follen (1787-1867)
and Eliza Cook (1816-89)

This is the farmer sowing the corn,
That kept the cock that crowed in the morn,
That waked the priest all shaven and shorn,
That married the man all tattered and torn,
That kissed the maiden all forlorn
That milked the cow with the crumpled horn,
That tossed the dog
That worried the cat
That killed the rat
That ate the malt
That lay in the house that Jack built.

There was a crooked man and he walked
a crooked mile,
He found a crooked sixpence against a
crooked stile.
He bought a crooked cat, which caught a
crooked mouse,
And they all lived together in a little
crooked house.

Nursery Rhymes J.O. Halliwell (1820-89)

Sing, sing, what shall I sing?
The cat's run away with the pudding string:
Do, do, what shall I do?
The cat has bitten it quite in two!

A cat came fiddling out of a barn,
With a pair of bagpipes under her arm;
She could sing nothing but "Fiddle cum fee,
The mouse has married the bumble bee."
Pipe Cat, Dance Mouse;
We'll have a wedding at our good house.

### The Owl And The Pussy Cat

The Owl and the Pussy-cat went to sea
    In a beautiful pea-green boat:
They took some honey, and plenty of money
    Wrapped up in a five-pound note.
The Owl looked up to the stars above,
    And sang to a small guitar,
"O lovely Pussy, O Pussy, my love,
    What a beautiful pussy you are!"

Pussy said to the Owl, "You elegant fowl,
    How charmingly sweet you sing!
Oh! let us be married; too long have we have tarried:
    But what shall we do for a ring?"
They sailed away, for a year and a day,
    To the land where the bong-tree grows;
And there in a wood a Piggy-wig stood,
    With a ring in the end of his nose.

"Dear Pig, are you willing to sell for one shilling
        Your ring?" Said the Piggy, "I will."
So they took it away, and were married next day
        By the Turkey who lives on the hill.
They dined on mince, and slices of quince,
        Which they ate with a runcible spoon;*
And hand in hand, on the edge of the sand
        They danced by the light of the moon,
        The moon, the moon,
They danced by the light of the moon.

                        Edward Lear (1812-88)


(*Runcible spoon: a term coined by Lear and defined as a forklike
utensil with two broad prongs and one sharp, curved prong as used
for serving hors d'oeuvres.)

High diddle diddle
The cat and the fiddle.
The cow jumped over the moon;
The little dog laughed
To see such craft
and the dish ran away with the spoon.

Ding, dong, bell
Pussy's in the well;
Who put her in?
Little Tommy Green.
Who pulled her out?
Little Johnny Stout.

# Pussy At The Fireside

Pussy at the fireside
Sippin' pease brose;
Down came a cinder
and burnt pussy's nose.

"Oh," said Pussy
"That's not fair!"
"Oh," said the cinder
"You shouldnie been there!"

*Anonymous*

I know a little pussy,
Her coat is silver gray,
She lives out in the meadow,
She'll never run away.
She'll never be a cat,
For she's a pussy willow--
Now, what do you think of that?
    Meow, meow, meow, meow,
    Meow, meow, meow, meow,  SCAT!

*And finally Dear Cat Lovers:*

Let your boat of life be light,
packed with only what you need--
a homely home and simple pleasures,
one or two friends, worthy of the name,
someone to love and someone to love you,
a CAT, a dog, and a pipe or two,
enough to eat and enough to wear,
and a little more than enough to drink:
for thirst is a dangerous thing.

Jerome Klapka Jerome (1859-1927)

123

# Acknowledgments

*Every effort has been made to trace ownership of copyrighted material contained in this volume. Should a question arise from the use of any item, the publisher expresses regret and will be pleased to make the necessary correction in future editions.*

*Crown Publishing has granted permission for the use of "Cruel Clever Sally" found in <u>2715 One-Line Quotations for Speakers and Writers</u>, Edward F. Murphy, editor. Crown Publishing has granted permission for the use of "God created cat that man..." found in <u>The Crown Treasury of Relevant Quotations</u>, Edward F. Murphy, editor. Doubleday Publishing has granted permission for the use of "There was a young man who was bitten" and "There was a kind curate of Kew" found in <u>Lots of Limericks</u>, Louis Untermeyer, editor. Facts on File has granted permission for the use of "Whisper some kindly word to bless" found in <u>The Quotable Woman</u>. Templegate Publishers has granted permission for the use of "Kevin Barry" found in <u>A Book of Irish Quotations</u>. Halycon House has granted permission for the use of "Muse versus Mews" found in <u>Home and Holiday Verse</u>. The quotation by Dorothy Parker's friend, "Have you tried curiosity?" appears in <u>The Little,</u>*

<u>Brown Book of Quotations</u>.  The quotation by Ferdinand Mery, "God created the cat so..." appears in <u>The Crown Treasury Of Relevant Quotations</u>.  Carl Sandburg's poem, "The fog comes on little cat feet...", appears in Bartlett's <u>Familiar Quotations</u>.

Cats have found their way into the hearts of many, as evidenced by the tributes quoted in this book.  Not so long ago, I doubted that I could have any real affection for one.  However, Hugger has proved to be a fine friend, a worthy model, and an inspiration.  Everyone should have a Hugger in his life.

Thanks are due my family and friends for encouragement, Judy Yamada for pencil sketches, and MAX GORDON for his invaluable assistance and suggestions.

Campbell CA
September 1994

*Richard Gordon*

# INDEX

# GIFT COPIES

### Additional copies of this book are available from:

## Gordon Publishing
## 91 Jane Ann Way,
## Campbell CA 95008-2712

Please send ___ copies of <u>CATQUOTES</u> and Anecdotes, Etc., etc., etc.

to: Name(s)_____

Address_____

City/Zip_____

$12.95 ea. (tax included)_____

Shipping and handling $2.00 ea._____

Find enclosed check or money order for $ _____